A Note to Parents and Teachers

DK [...] [...] conjunction with leading literacy experts, [...] Cliff Moon M.Ed., Honorary Fellow of the University of Reading. Cliff Moon has spent many years as a teacher and teacher educator specializing in reading and has written more than 140 books for children and teachers. He reviews regularly for teachers' journals.

Beautiful illustrations and superb full-colour photographs combine with engaging, easy-to-read stories to offer a fresh approach to each subject in the series. Each DK READER is guaranteed to capture a child's interest while developing his or her reading skills, general knowledge, and love of reading.

The five levels of DK READERS are aimed at different reading abilities, enabling you to choose the books that are exactly right for your child:

Pre-level 1: Learning to read
Level 1: Beginning to read
Level 2: Beginning to read alone
Level 3: Reading alone
Level 4: Proficient readers

The "normal" age at which a child begins to read can be anywhere from three to eight years old, so these levels are only a general guideline.

No matter which level you select, you can be sure that you are helping your child learn to read, then read to learn!

DK

LONDON, NEW YORK, MUNICH,
MELBOURNE, and DEHLI

Series Editors Deborah Lock and Penny Smith
Art Editor Jacqueline Gooden
Production Alison Lenane
DTP Designer Almudena Díaz
Jacket Designer Hedi Gutt

Reading Consultant
Cliff Moon, M.Ed.

Published in Great Britain by
Dorling Kindersley Limited
80 Strand, London WC2R ORL
2 4 6 8 10 9 7 5 3

A Penguin Company

A CIP record for this book is available
from the British Library

ISBN-13: 978-1-4053-1111-3

Colour reproduction by Colourscan, Singapore
Printed and bound in China by L Rex Printing Co., Ltd.

The publisher would like to thank the following for their kind permission
to reproduce their photographs:
a=above; c=centre; b=below; l=left; r=right t=top

Alamy Images: Gabe Palmer III 4-5; Photofusion Picture Library/ Molly Cooper
15c; Hemera Technologies 25bcl; image100 27; ImageDJ 29. **Corbis:** 10br;
Ariel Skelley 28; Cat Gwynn 24-25; John Henley 30-31; Keren Su 7; Tom Stewart
16-17; Wartenberg/Picture Press 14. **Early Learning Centre:** 7bcr, 10tl, 10bl, 11bl,
12br, 13cr, 13bl, 18bcr, 20br, 20t, 21br, 22c, 25bcr. **Getty Images:** Patrick Molnar 6;
Sean Murphy 26; Terry Vine 21. **Photolibrary.com:** Studio 10 -Scholastic 11.
Zefa Visual Media: E. Krenkel 18-19; Meeke 12t; R. Elstermann 9t; R.de Rooij 23.

All other images © Dorling Kindersley
For more information see: www.dkimages.com

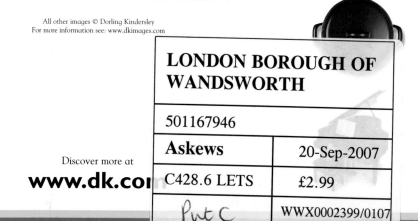

Discover more at

www.dk.com

DK READERS

LEARNING
pre-level **1**
TO READ

Let's Make
Music

DK

A Dorling Kindersley Book

bin lid

We are making music
as we march.

cymbal

cymbals

We are clashing cymbals
to make a loud noise.

drumstick

drum

drums

We are banging
on drums
to make the beat.

bell

We are
shaking
the bells
to make
them ring.

bells

xylophone

We are hitting the keys to make a tune.

xylophones

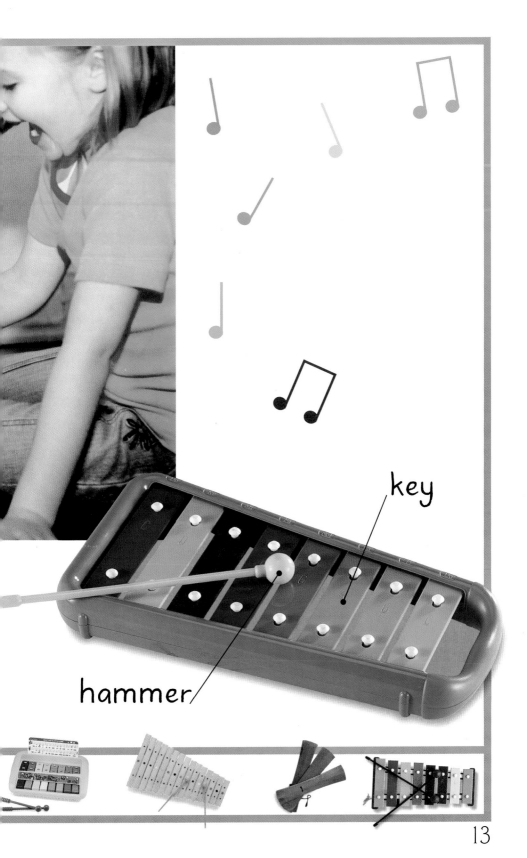

key

hammer

whistle

whistles

We are blowing
our whistles
at the carnival.

carnival

I am hitting the pans with spoons.

 pans

spoon

lid

17

I am playing
high and low notes
on the keyboard.

 keyboards

keyboard

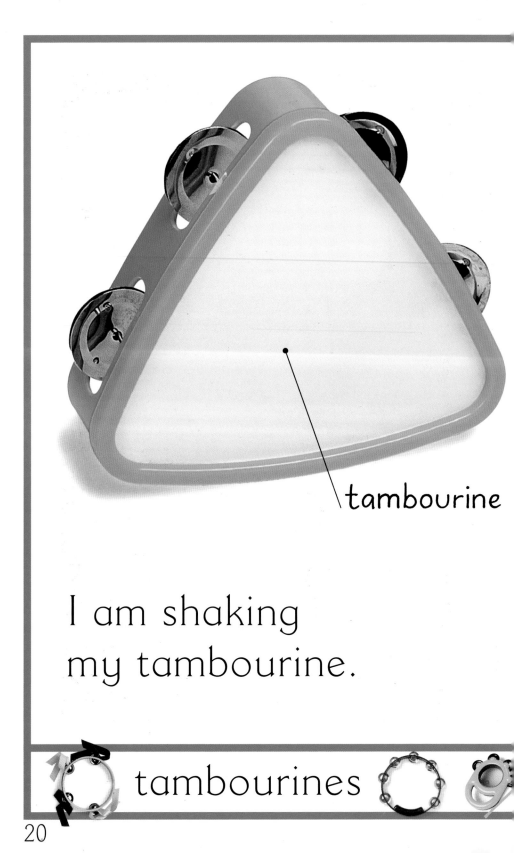

tambourine

I am shaking
my tambourine.

tambourines

I am strumming
the strings
on my guitar.

fret

string

guitars

guitar

23

I am blowing notes on my mouth organ.

 mouth organs

mouth organ

Let's clap our hands and sing.

hands

feet

Let's move our feet
and dance.

Let's all play

music together.

Picture word list

cymbal

page 6

drum

page 8

bell

page 10

xylophone

page 12

whistle

page 14

pan

page 16

keyboard

page 18

tambourine

page 20

guitar

page 22

mouth organ

page 24

hands

page 26

feet

page 28